Drake Bell and Josh Peck

Joanne Mattern

P.O. Box 196
Hockessin, Delaware 19707
Visit us on the web: www.mitchelllane.com
Comments? email us: mitchelllane@mitchelllane.com

Mitchell Lane PUBLISHERS

Printing   1   2   3   4   5   6   7   8   9

A Robbie Reader
Contemporary Biography/Science Biography

Albert Einstein	Albert Pujols	Alex Rodriguez
Aly and AJ	Amanda Bynes	Brittany Murphy
Charles Schulz	Dakota Fanning	Dale Earnhardt Jr.
Donovan McNabb	**Drake Bell & Josh Peck**	Dr. Seuss
Dylan & Cole Sprouse	Henry Ford	Hilary Duff
Jamie Lynn Spears	Jessie McCartney	Johnny Gruelle
LeBron James	Mandy Moore	Mia Hamm
Miley Cyrus	Philo T. Farnsworth	Raven Symone
Robert Goddard	Shaquille O'Neal	The Story of Harley-Davidson
Syd Hoff	Tiki Barber	Thomas Edison
Tony Hawk		

Library of Congress Cataloging-in-Publication Data
Mattern, Joanne, 1963-
    Drake Bell and Josh Peck / by Joanne Mattern.
        p. cm. — (A Robbie reader)
    Includes bibliographical references and index.
    ISBN-13: 978-1-58415-592-8 (library bound)
    1. Bell, Drake, 1986– —Juvenile literature. 2. Peck, Josh, 1986– —Juvenile literature.
3. Actors—United States—Biography—Juvenile literature. I. Title.
PN2287.B413M38 2008
792.02'80922—dc22
                                                                                2007023488

ABOUT THE AUTHOR: Joanne Mattern is the author of more than 200 nonfiction books for children. Along with biographies, she has written extensively about animals, nature, history, sports, and foreign cultures. She wrote *Brian McBride, Peyton Manning, Miguel Tejada,* and *Tiki Barber* for Mitchell Lane Publishers. She lives near New York City with her husband and four children.

PHOTO CREDITS: Cover—Coverup/Globe Photos; pp. 4, 20—Jeffrey Mayer/WireImage; pp. 6, 7—AP Photo/Reed Saxon; p. 8—Gary Gershof/WireImage; p. 10—Robin Dodson; pp. 11, 14, 25, 26—Globe Photos; pp. 12, 16—Frazer Harrison/Getty Images; p. 15—Eric Neitzel/WireImage; p. 18—Kevin Mazur/WireImage; pp. 19, 27—Nickelodeon; p. 22—Jesse Grant/WireImage.

TABLE OF CONTENTS

Drake Bell and Josh Peck are two of Nickelodeon's hottest stars. When they first met, they didn't think they'd get along at all.

Not Love at First Sight

Josh Peck was excited. The thirteen-year-old actor had just gotten a part on *The Amanda Show* on the television **network** Nickelodeon.

When Josh went to the show's set, he got a nasty surprise. He found out that another thirteen-year-old, Drake Bell, was already on the show. Josh and Drake had met before. They had both been on a Nickelodeon game show called *Double Dare*. At that time, they had not gotten along with each other. "We didn't hit it off at all," Drake said. "I don't know why, but we just kind of rubbed each other the wrong way."

Josh did not like Drake either. He thought Drake was too cool and **confident** (KON-fih-dent). Josh also felt that he was not as good-looking as Drake. The two had nothing in common. Still, they had to work together on the television show.

Josh Peck listens to director Fred Savage on the set of *Drake and Josh*, while a makeup artist does a last-minute touch-up.

As Drake and Josh worked together, a funny thing happened. They started to like each other. Even though they were very different, they worked well together. Soon they were good friends.

Fans liked Drake and Josh too. So did Nickelodeon. The network decided that they

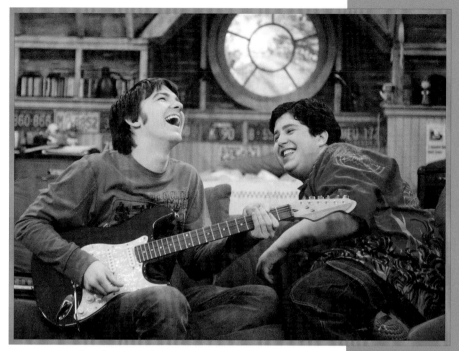

Drake Bell (left) and Josh Peck have some fun on the set of their television show.

should have their own show. In 2004, *Drake and Josh* began on Nickelodeon. The show was about two boys who become stepbrothers. Like the real Drake and Josh, the two characters on the show were very different from each other. Like the real Drake and Josh, the two characters become a great team!

Drake shows his musical talent on MTV's *Total Request Live* in December 2006. He describes his music as "very Beatles, Beach Boys, but with a very modern sound. I'm a huge fan of the Beatles, the Beach Boys, Buddy Holly, and Elvis Presley."

All About Drake

Jared Drake Bell was born on June 27, 1986, in Newport Beach, California. He has two older brothers, Robert and Travis. Their parents, Joe Bell and Robin Dodson, divorced when Drake was young. He lived with his mother and stepfather, Roy. Drake's mother is a world champion **billiards** (BILL-yurdz) player.

Drake always loved acting. He started taking acting classes when he was just five years old. When he was eight, he got to be on television for the first time. Drake appeared on the hit **comedy** (KAH-muh-dee) series *Home Improvement*. He also made some television commercials and appeared on other television shows, including *Seinfeld* and *The Drew Carey Show*.

Drake's mother, Robin Dodson, is in the Billiards Congress of America's Hall of Fame. Although Drake learned how to play the game, he says he isn't very good at it. "You wouldn't expect that my mom is who she is if you saw me play. At all."

In 1995, nine-year-old Drake appeared in his first movie, called *Drifting School*. He had a very small part in it. The next year, he appeared in *Jerry Maguire*. This movie starred Tom Cruise and was a huge hit!

In 1999, Drake appeared in a made-for-TV movie called *The Jack Bull*. He did so well that he was **nominated** (NAH-mih-nay-ted) for the Young

In 1999, Drake (left) played Cage Redding in the western *The Jack Bull.* Other cast members were Miranda Otto and John Cusack (who played his parents) and Jon McGinley (right).

Artist Award for Best Performance in a TV Movie or Pilot.

Drake also loved music. When he was thirteen, he started taking guitar lessons. His teacher was rock star Roger Daltrey from the legendary group The Who. The two met when they made a movie together called *Chasing Destiny.* Soon Drake was singing and writing songs, too.

By 1999, Drake was a busy young man. His life was about to get even busier!

Josh was so successful as a preteen comedian, his mother insisted that they move to California, where Josh could go to performing arts school. She said, "All this great luck and good fortune is raining on you. We have to go."

Being Josh

Joshua Michael Peck grew up on the other side of the country from Drake Bell. He was born on November 10, 1986, in New York City. Josh's parents were not married, and he never knew his father. He grew up in a tiny apartment with his mother, Barbara. "Money was scarce," Josh later told *USA Today*. "Sometimes I'd have the couch, she'd have the bed, and then we'd switch off."

Josh was a lonely child. He has a medical condition called **asthma** (AZ-muh). A person with asthma has trouble breathing. Because of his illness, Josh could not always play outside. Instead, he spent a lot of time watching old television shows. He liked comedies the best, and admired comedians like Bill Cosby. Soon Josh decided to do comedy himself. He began telling jokes at home and at school.

Josh (far right), who was bullied as a child, plays a bully in the movie *Mean Creek*. From left to right are cast mates Rory Culkin, Trevor Morgan, Carly Schroeder, Scott Mechlowicz, and Ryan Kelly.

Being funny helped Josh deal with another problem. He was overweight and was often teased and bullied by other children. He soon learned that telling jokes made life easier. "If I thought a kid was going to make fun of me, I might make fun of myself first," he explained to *USA Today*.

When Josh was eight years old, he began performing in comedy clubs around New York City. Josh's young age and funny jokes got the

In 2005, Josh had fun coloring with a young hospital patient, Courtney, as part of a Spice Up the Fight Against Childhood Cancer charity event. The event raised money for St. Jude Children's Research Hospital. "It's basically about bringing awareness to such an amazing cause, in something that has helped people for years now. Any way that I can be a part of it, I feel really privileged to be able to do that," says Josh.

attention of casting directors for the Nickelodeon television network. In 1999, they offered him a role on *The Amanda Show*. Josh and his mother moved to California. Josh was going to be a TV star!

The cast of *Drake and Josh* (from left to right): Jonathan Goldstein, Nancy Sullivan, Drake Bell, Josh Peck, and Miranda Cosgrove. In the show, Miranda's character, Megan, is constantly creating trouble for the boys.

Amanda Meets Drake and Josh

In 1999, *The Amanda Show,* starring the teenaged Amanda Bynes, was one of the most popular shows on Nickelodeon. It was made up of sketch comedy. Instead of telling one story, each show featured shorter pieces, with teen actors doing funny things. A sketch might last only a few minutes. Teen and preteen fans loved it. The show was fast, funny, and a little bit crazy.

Drake and Josh were also busy making movies. In 2000, Josh appeared in *Snow Day.* In 2001, he starred in *Max Keeble's Big Move.* Both of these movies were aimed at families and preteens. They were very successful. Meanwhile, Drake appeared in the movies *High Fidelity* and *Perfect Game.*

Amanda Bynes, Drake, and Josh worked together on the hilarious *Amanda Show*. That program launched the careers of all three young actors.

The *Amanda Show* ended in 2002. Nickelodeon still wanted Drake and Josh to be on their television network. In 2004, the show *Drake and Josh* went on the air. Soon it was one of the most popular programs on Nickelodeon.

On the show, the two teens appear as Drake Parker and Josh Nichols. Like the real Drake and Josh, the two characters are very different from each other. The show's producer, Dan Schneider, told the *Chicago Sun-Times* that Josh is "a funny kid who is sometimes a little awkward." Schneider says Drake, on the other hand, is "the kid every young kid wants to be."

Both Drake and Josh love being on the show. Both enjoy their characters and the theme of the show. Drake describes it as being about

The show *Drake and Josh* follows the funny adventures of two stepbrothers. It became so popular, full-length movies have been made for the pair.

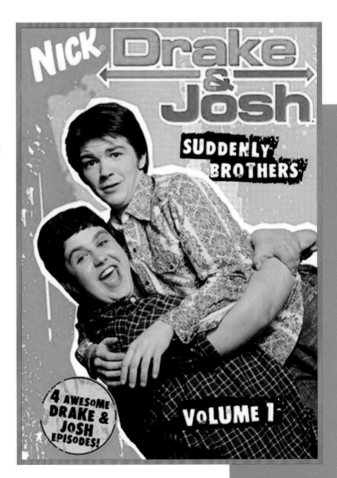

Drake and Josh get along well together even when they're not working.

"friendship and how these two different people get along."

Drake also got to use his talent for music on the show. He wrote and performed the theme song and often plays guitar and sings on the show.

Drake and Josh have become great friends. They often spend time together after work. "It's funny," Drake told *Girls' Life* magazine in 2006. "We work all day long from eight in the morning until eight at night. So at the end of the day, Josh is like, 'Hey, what are you doing tonight?' We see each other all day and still want to hang out after work."

Drake and Josh's close friendship has made them a great team. It would also help Drake face the biggest **crisis** (CRY-sis) of his life.

Drake and Josh became so popular, it won the Kids' Choice Award for Favorite Television Show in 2006. Drake also won that year for Favorite TV Actor. He would score a second Favorite TV Actor Blimp in 2007.

After the Crash

On December 29, 2005, Drake and a friend were driving home from the beach in Malibu, California. Drake was driving an old car that did not have shoulder straps on the seat belts. He was stopped to make a turn when another car smashed into them. His face crashed into the hard steering wheel. He lost seven teeth. Even worse, he broke his jaw in three places, and also a bone in his neck.

Drake had several operations (op-uh-RAY-shunz) on his neck and jaw. His jaw was wired shut for almost two months. He was afraid that his acting career was over. He told *People Weekly*, "My stitched-up gash looked like someone took a live caterpillar and stuck it on my chin."

Josh would not let Drake feel sorry for himself. Drake told *People*, "Josh was like, 'You're still better-looking than me.' Josh was bringing me smoothies every day. It was so much more than I would expect. He was totally awesome."

After Drake's jaw was unwired, he really wanted to go back to work. Nickelodeon wanted him back, too. *Drake and Josh* started taping again on March 8, 2006. "The accident showed me how much I love what I'm doing and that it can be taken away in a split second," he said.

Josh also faced big changes in 2005 and 2006. After being overweight all his life, he decided it was time to slim down. He worked with a trainer and used exercise and a healthy diet to lose weight. He lost over 100 pounds! Josh told the *Chicago Sun-Times* that he lost weight for a good reason. "It was about being happy in my own skin and having a healthier outlook on life," he said.

By 2007, Drake and Josh were still going strong on their TV show. Meanwhile, they had made many movie appearances too. Josh won excellent **reviews** (ree-VYOOZ) in 2004 when he appeared in a film called *Mean Creek*. In the movie, Josh plays an overweight teen who becomes a bully to cover up his unhappiness about himself. Since he had grown up overweight, Josh felt a special closeness to his character.

In 2006, Josh appeared in an **independent** (in-duh-PEN-dunt) film called *Special*. He also provided the voice for Eddie in the **animated** (AA-nih-may-ted) comedy *Ice Age: The Meltdown.*

Josh provided the voice of Eddie in the 2006 movie *Ice Age: The Meltdown.* He loved this role, saying, "It was fantastic. . . . I rediscovered the fact [that] I had a vivid imagination. . . . I asked them to crank up the air conditioning so I felt genuinely cold and then I would blast off."

Rene Russo (left) plays the part of a widow with ten kids in the 2005 movie *Yours, Mine, and Ours*. Drake (third from the right) plays one of her children. As in *Drake and Josh*, Miranda Cosgrove (seated on couch, left) plays one of his sisters.

In 2005, Drake appeared in the movie *Yours, Mine and Ours*, starring Dennis Quaid. He also put more attention into his musical career. In September that year he released the album *Telegraph*. In 2006, he released another album, called *It's Only Time*. He would tour with NextFest in the summer of 2007 to promote the album.

Drake and Josh also have a bright future together as their characters from the television

Drake and Josh continued their comedy adventures in the 2006 television movie *Drake and Josh Go Hollywood.*

show. In 2006, Drake and Josh starred in the television movie *Drake and Josh Go Hollywood.* At least three more *Drake and Josh* television movies were planned for 2007, including *Drake and Josh in New York!*

Both Drake and Josh know they are very lucky. They star in a popular TV show and are able to do the things they love best—acting and playing music. Most of all, the two friends are able to work together as a popular comedy team.

1986 Jared Drake Bell is born in Newport Beach, California, on June 27. Joshua Michael Peck is born in New York City on November 10.

1994 Drake appears in his first television show, *Home Improvement*.

1996 Josh begins appearing in comedy clubs around New York City.

1999 Drake and Josh appear on *The Amanda Show*.

2004 Drake and Josh star in their own television show, *Drake and Josh*; Josh appears in the movie *Mean Creek*.

2005 Josh begins to lose weight through diet and exercise; Drake releases his first album, *Telegraph*; Drake breaks his jaw in a car accident on December 29.

2006 Drake goes back to work in March; *Drake and Josh* is named Favorite Television Show and Drake wins Favorite TV Actor at the Kids' Choice Awards; *Drake and Josh Go Hollywood* is released; Drake releases his second album, *It's Only Time*.

2007 Drake is again named Favorite Television Actor at the Kids' Choice Awards; *Drake and Josh in New York* is scheduled for release, along with several other Drake and Josh projects; Drake goes on tour to promote his album.

FILMOGRAPHY

Drake Bell
2007 *College*
2005 *Yours, Mine and Ours*
2001 *Chasing Destiny*
2000 *Perfect Game*
High Fidelity
1999 *The Jack Bull*
Dragonworld: The Legend Continues
Dill Scallion
1996 *Jerry Maguire*
1995 *The Neon Bible*
Drifting School
1999–
2001 *The Amanda Show* (TV Series)

Josh Peck
2007 *American Primitive*
Drillbit Taylor
2006 *Ice Age: The Meltdown*
2004 *Mean Creek*
2001 *Max Keeble's Big Move*
2000 *Snow Day*
The Newcomers
2000–
2002 *The Amanda Show* (TV Series)

Together
2007 *Drake and Josh in New York!*
2006 *Drake and Josh Go Hollywood*
2004 *Drake and Josh* (TV series)

DISCOGRAPHY

Drake Bell
2006 *It's Only Time*
2005 *Telegraph*

Books

While there are no other books about Drake or Josh currently available, you might enjoy these books in our Robbie Readers series:

Leavitt, Amie Jane. *Amanda Bynes*. Hockessin, Delaware: Mitchell Lane Publishers, 2008.

————. *Dylan and Cole Sprouse*. Hockessin, Delaware: Mitchell Lane Publishers, 2008.

Tracy, Kathleen. *Aly and AJ*. Hockessin, Delaware: Mitchell Lane Publishers, 2008.

Works Consulted

"Drake Bell." *Girls' Life*, February/March 2004, volume 10, issue 4, p. 39.

Ingrassia, Lisa. "Crash and Learn." *People Weekly*, April 10, 2006, volume 65, issue 14, p. 105.

"Josh Peck Talks *Ice Age: The Meltdown*," Movieweb.com, March 25, 2006, http://www.movieweb.com/news/11/11811.php

Keck, William. "Josh Peck Lightens Up." *USA Today*, August 26, 2004.

"Peck's Pounds." *Scholastic Choices*, September 2006, volume 22, issue 1, p. 4.

"Q and A: Drake Bell." *Know Your World Extra*, November 3, 2006, volume 40, issue 4, p. 4.

"Ring a Bell?" *Kids Tribute*, Fall 2004, volume 16, issue 3, p. 7.

Rogers, John. " 'Drake and Josh' Channeling Martin and Lewis." *Chicago Sun-Times*, October 13, 2006.

————. " 'Drake and Josh' Make Perfect TV Couple." *Chicago Sun-Times*, May 14, 2004.

White, Kelly. "Nothin' Fake About Drake." *Girls' Life*, February 2006, volume 12, issue 4, pp. 42–43.

Zwiker, Jason A. "Celebrity Shots: Drake Bell." Originally published in *Pool & Billiard Magazine,* May 2006; http://www.zwiker.com/drake.htm

On the Internet
Drake Bell Fan Page
http://www.popstarsplus.com/actors_drakebell.htm
Josh Peck Fan Site
http://www.josh-peck.net
Official Drake Bell Website
http://www.drakebell.com

GLOSSARY

animated (AA-nih-may-ted)—movies made using drawings instead of real people or animals.

asthma (AZ-muh)—a condition that makes it hard to breathe.

billiards (BIL-yurdz)—a game such as pool in which a cue stick is used to hit balls into pockets around a table.

comedy (KAH-muh-dee)—something that makes people laugh.

confident (KON-fih-dent)—having a strong belief in someone's abilities.

crisis (CRY-sis)—something that could cause an unwanted change.

independent (in-duh-PEN-dunt)—in movies, free from the control of a major studio.

network (NET-wurk)—a group of television stations.

nominated (NAH-mih-nay-tud)—chosen.

reviews (reev-YOOZ)—pieces of writing that say whether something is good or bad and why.